HÄGAR
THE HORRIBLE
Dik Browne

Game for Anything

EGMONT

introducing...

HAGAR THE HORRIBLE
a hard-working Barbarian businessman. He's in sacking and looting.

His wife, **HELGA**. She finds civilizing Hagar a 24-hour-a-day job!

This is **HAMLET**, their son, a real problem child! He insists on wearing his hair short, bathing, reading and otherwise behaving in a very unbarbarian manner.

HONI, their daughter, is sixteen years old, and still not married!

But that's not the end of Hagar's troubles... there's also **LUCKY EDDIE** who must be the most hopeless assistant in history!

All rights reserved under International and Pan-American Copyright Conventions. No portion of this work may be reproduced by any process without the publisher's permission.

Copyright © 1980 by King Features, New York/Bulls, Frankfurt a.M. and Ehapa Verlag GmbH
Copyright © 1980 Egmont Publishing Limited

First published in Great Britain by Egmont Publishing Limited, 70 Old Compton Street, London W1V 5PA

Printed and bound in Great Britain by
©ollins, Glasgow.

ISBN 0 86173 033 X